ANIMALS OF THE RAINFOREST

Wildlife of the Jungle
Encyclopedias for Children

SPEEDY
PUBLISHING

Speedy Publishing LLC
40 E. Main St. #1156
Newark, DE 19711
www.speedypublishing.com

Rainforests are forests that experience a high level of rainfall. The Amazon rainforest is the largest tropical rainforest in the world.

Spider monkeys live in wet and dense tropical rainforests. Spider monkeys spend their life in the treetops and they can be rarely seen on the ground.

Spider monkeys are named that way because they hang from the trees by holding different branches with their limbs and long tails.

Sloths live in the jungles and rainforests of Central and South America.

Sloths have round face, sad eyes, small ears and short tail. Their body is covered with wiry fur.

The capybara is the largest of all living rodents. Capybaras can weigh as much as 175 lbs.

Capybaras are semi-aquatic, spending a lot of time in the water. Capybaras can live 8-10 years in the wild.

Toucans are native to southern Mexico in Central America, the northern areas of South America.

Toucans don't like to fly. When they need to leave the safety of trees, they will glide through the air and travel small distances.

Jaguars are only found in the Americas. Jaguars can weigh 200-250 pounds and reach 5-7 feet in length.

Jaguars are nocturnal and solitary animals. Jaguars mark their territory with their waste or by clawing trees.

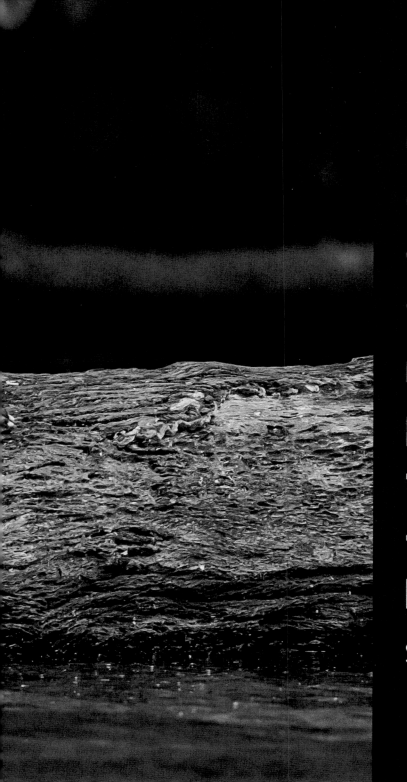

Giant river otters live in family groups which include monogamous parents and the offspring from several breeding seasons.

Giant otters have dense, velvety and thick brown fur which is water repellent. Giant otters are excellent swimmers.

Poison Dart frogs live in rainforests in Central and South America. They can be found in trees, as well as under leaves and logs.

Poison dart frogs got their name because some Amerindian tribes have used their secretions to poison their darts.

The Green Anaconda is the largest snake in the world. The Green Anaconda lives in South America.

Anacondas are constrictors. Anacondas will grab its victim wrap its body around the prey and squeeze it until it dies from suffocation.

The harpy eagle is one of the largest eagles in the world. Harpy Eagles are carnivores and are the apex predators in their environment.

They are typically found throughout Mexico and parts of Central and South America.